IMAGES
of America

FERRIES OF
PUGET SOUND

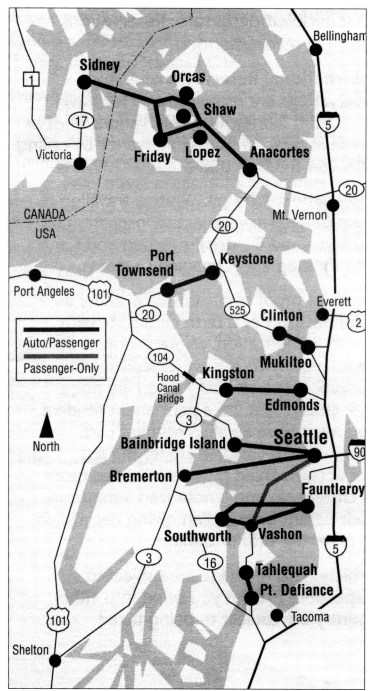

This is a modern map of the Puget Sound area, listing the ferry routes. (Courtesy of Washington State Ferries.)

On the Cover: The jaunty little *Kitsap* (1925) served smaller runs such as Mukilteo–Columbia Beach and Point Defiance–Tahlequah for both Black Ball and Washington State Ferries. She was retired in 1961. (Author's collection.)

IMAGES
of America

FERRIES OF
PUGET SOUND

Steven J. Pickens

ARCADIA
PUBLISHING

Published by Arcadia Publishing
Charleston SC, Chicago IL, Portsmouth NH, San Francisco CA

Printed in the United States of America

Library of Congress Catalog Card Number: 2005934861

For all general information contact Arcadia Publishing at:
Telephone 843-853-2070
Fax 843-853-0044
E-mail sales@arcadiapublishing.com
For customer service and orders:
Toll-Free 1-888-313-2665

Visit us on the Internet at www.arcadiapublishing.com

*For Mom and Dad, who always encouraged me
and have been there for me when I needed them.*

CONTENTS

ACKNOWLEDGMENTS

I would like to thank all those who aided me in the completion of this project and helped make this book possible. Without their help and photographs, a complete portrait of the ferries could not have been possible. Thanks in particular go to Indra Black, Brandon Moser, Richard Moser, Tom Sanislo, Patti Lander, Ross Williams, Khristopher La Plante, John S. Kwant, Debbie Lund, Jean P. Hudson, Washington State Ferries, and David Ruble for either donating or taking photographs of the boats to contribute, and to Joe Thompson for giving Julie Albright, editor at Arcadia, my name for a possible ferryboat book.

Special thanks must go to the Museum of History and Industry's Carolyn Marr, who rescued me in my hunt for photographs of the Washington State Ferries short-timer, the motor vessel (M/V) *Rosario*. Without her and the excellent staff at MOHAI, keepers of the famed Joe Williamson maritime photograph collection, the book would have had a rather large hole in it.

INTRODUCTION

Ferryboats have been a way of life on Puget Sound for decades. In the years since the State of Washington took over operations from the Puget Sound Navigation Company in 1951, the fleet has retained its eclectic qualities. The wooden vessels of the early years may be gone, but commuters and crew alike recognize each boat for their individual personality and lay claim, sometimes fiercely, to "their" boats. Few would argue, for example, that the *Klahowya*, sailing at Vashon since her construction in 1958, is a "Vashon boat," or that the *Cathlamet* and *Kittitas*, sisters of the Issaquah class, have been "Mukilteo boats" (as they have rarely left the run since their debut).

Appearing on countless postcards, photographs, and souvenirs, the ferryboats of Puget Sound are not only the state's number-one tourist attraction, but are also cultural symbols of the region. Residents are proud of the ferryboats and protect them ardently. They are floating highways, places for meeting friends, doing work, or sharing stories. They have been the settings for every stage of life, from weddings to a few births when there wasn't quite enough time to get to the mainland, and even for a final good-bye to those who have passed, with ashes scattered from the stern.

Far more than a mere method of transport, the ferries of Puget Sound became a friend for residents. More than one tear has been shed when they become too old and are retired. Names like *Vashon*, *Kalakala*, and *Chetzemoka* still resonate with fondness and nostalgia long after their profiles have vanished from the horizon.

The diverse fleet of Washington State Ferries today consists of 28 vessels. Four ferries came from San Francisco Bay and were constructed at the time when Lindbergh flew solo across the Atlantic. One lone ferry once sailed the waters of Chesapeake Bay, far from Puget Sound. Three were the first built for the state and are now receiving gold stripes on their funnels for 50 years of service. One tiny little 40-car boat was built specially to sail the shortest crossing on the Sound. Four fast and sleek sisters ended the 1960s, retiring a handful of old, inefficient boats. Two mammoths built in the early 1970s became emblems of Seattle. Six more closed out the decade and became legendary for their initial problems. Four passenger-only boats were built to stem the tide of cars on the ever-crowded highways. Finally, three gargantuan ferries were constructed in the late 1990s to become the largest double-ended ferries ever built.

On the cusp of great changes, Washington State Ferries will be adding up to five boats over the next decade to pension off some of the oldest working ferries in the world. Soon the names familiar to generations of travelers in the state will pass into memory. At this pivotal moment in the progress of the region's marine highways, it is appropriate as the area moves into the future to take a look back at the past and bid Puget Sound's "ancient mariners" a fond farewell.

In these pages, a photographic record of the gentle giants of Puget Sound can be found as they once were and are today—the icons of region and a familiar sight to generations of travelers on inland water highways of the state.

The fledgling service begins, as this c. 1959 brochure from the Washington State Ferries demonstrates. (Author's collection.)

One

THE GHOST FLEET

The Washington State Ferries (WSF) has never scrapped a vessel. Even the venerable *Lincoln* of 1908, which was listed as part of the fleet when the state took over operations in June of 1951, was sold to another owner before being dismantled.

Ferries, like people, have a lifespan. Running on an average of 16 hours daily, with only a few weeks off each year for maintenance, takes a tremendous toll on hulls, machinery, and equipment. On average, a ferryboat will last 40 years. With good preventative maintenance and refurbishing, they can run much longer.

When taking over from Capt. Alexander Peabody's Puget Sound Navigation Company (or Black Ball Line) in 1951, the state inherited an eclectic fleet that included converted passenger steamers, vessels made completely of wood, and a streamlined silver ferry that looked like it was out of a *Buck Rogers* movie serial. The newest vessel was 16 years old, and much of the fleet had been designed for the slim cars of the 1920s and 1930s. Tailfins were already starting to sprout on Cadillacs and the true behemoths of the 1950s were a mere few years away. Thus, the state put into effect a policy that remains in place today—rebuild and modernize when practical, retire and sell when it isn't.

Many vessels of the Black Ball Line survived well into the 1970s, but the state began modernizing and expanding immediately. In September 1951, they retired and sold their first ferry, just three months into operations. In the following years, two newer ferries would be added and three would be built. One by one, the older vessels began to vanish from the Sound.

The Ghost Fleet of Washington State Ferries is well remembered by decades of travelers from the first to be retired and sold in 1951, the *Rosario*, to the most recent sale, the *Tyee*, in 2003. While most of these ferries are mere memories now, some remarkably survive and are enjoying a comfortable retirement.

The tiny *Rosario*, seen here in the 1930s, had originally been built as a much smaller steam ferry in 1923. Reconstructed and expanded in 1931 as a diesel-powered vessel, the ferry featured a full-service dining room and an elegant passenger cabin for travelers sailing from Anacortes to Bellingham and onto Sidney, British Columbia. (Photograph by Joe Williamson; courtesy of the Puget Sound Maritime Historical Society.)

Whittled down to a mere 33 cars, the *Rosario* was expensive to operate and inefficient. When the Agate Pass Bridge opened, her route from Suquamish to Indianola, then onto Seattle, was discontinued. Sold in September 1951, the ferry was converted into a cannery along the banks of the Snohomish River in Everett. Completely silted in later years, her superstructure was removed and the hull built over. The *Rosario* was built in 1923 (reconstructed in 1931) in Dockton, Washington. The ferry was made of wood, was 155 feet, 8 inches by 40 feet, 8 inches, and was powered by a diesel engine. (Photograph by Joe Williamson; courtesy of the Puget Sound Maritime Historical Society.)

The SS *Shasta*, pictured here in her original service on San Francisco Bay in the 1930s, was mainly used as a reserve boat. Brought to Puget Sound in 1941, she and her sister, *San Mateo*, oddly enough were not given Chinook jargon names as all the other transfers from San Francisco had. (Author's collection.)

The WSF retired the *Shasta* in 1959. She operated for a while on the Columbia River as the *Centennial Queen*, but her steam power plant proved too costly to run. It was later removed, and the vessel was extensively rebuilt as the *River Queen* in the early 1960s, a stationary restaurant that operated in the Portland area successfully into the 1990s. (Author's collection.)

This is the *Shasta* as she looks today. Unable to find permanent moorage, the ferry sits in Gobel, Oregon, waiting for someone to develop her. She was built in 1922 by Bethlehem Shipbuilding Corporation, San Francisco. The hull was constructed of steel with a wooden superstructure, and the vessel measures 216 feet, 7 inches by 63 feet, 8 inches. She was powered by a triple-expansion steam engine. (Courtesy of Patti Lander.)

Motor Vessel (M/V) *Kitsap* of 1925, seen here in the 1950s, was originally built for the Kitsap County Transportation Company, which was later taken over by the Black Ball Line. She sailed for Washington State Ferries until 1962, when she was sold to the State of Oregon for use between Megler, Washington, and Astoria, Oregon. When the Astoria Bridge was finished in 1966, the *Kitsap* was sold and taken to Alaska to be turned into a crab-processing plant, but sank under tow in Alaska in 1967. She was built by Lake Washington Shipyard at Houghton, Washington, in 1925 and was made completely of wood. She measured 165 feet, 7 inches by 50 feet, 5 inches and was powered by a Washington Estep diesel engine. (Courtesy of Washington State Ferries.)

The *Chippewa* is seen here, as originally built in 1900 as a passenger steamer. Constructed for service on the Great Lakes, she was purchased by the Puget Sound Navigation Company in 1907, sailing around the "horn" of South America to reach Puget Sound. (Author's collection.)

OLYMPIC PENINSULA
VICTORIA
and the
SANJUANISLANDS

BLACK BALL FERRIES
PUGET SOUND NAVIGATION COMPANY

Extensively rebuilt as a car ferry in 1926, the *Chippewa* became the flagship of the fleet. Capable of carrying 90 1926-sized cars and 2,000 passengers, she was at the time the largest ferry on Puget Sound, and was heavily promoted by Black Ball, appearing on nearly every brochure produced by the company at that time. (Author's collection.)

The *Chippewa* replaced the *Rosario* as the International ferry to Sidney, British Columbia. Remodeled in 1932, the ferry emerged with one smoke stack, a Busch-Sulzer diesel engine, and a passenger cabin paneled in Philippine mahogany. Amenities included a ladies' lounge, a men's smoking room, and a full-service lunch counter located amidships. Pictured here in the 1940s at the Sidney dock, she is backed in nearing departure time for Anacortes. (Courtesy of Brandon Moser.)

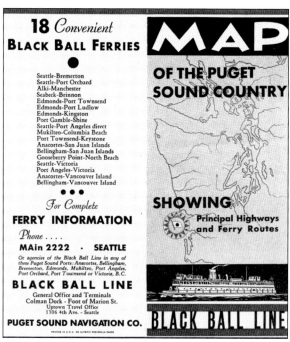

Before the days of the *Kalakala*, the *Chippewa* appeared on nearly all of the Black Ball Line's promotional materials. With budgets being stretched tight during the Depression, actual photographs of the ferry were replaced with stylized drawings, such as the one that appears on this map and brochure. (Author's collection.)

Pictured here in the early 1960s, the *Chippewa* glides through Rich Passage. By 1964, the ferry had become too expensive to run. Her hull upgrades proving exorbitantly expensive, and with a nine-foot, six-inch clearance on her car deck rendering her unable to haul any large trucks, the state wisely decided to retire her. She was to be turned into a maritime museum in San Francisco, but arsonists set her ablaze in 1968 and she was completely gutted. The *Chippewa* was originally built by Craig Shipbuilding, of Toledo, Ohio, in 1900. The vessel was rebuilt as a ferry by Lake Washington Shipyard, of Houghton, Washington, in 1926 and 1932. She had a steel hull and wooden superstructure, and measured 212 feet, 3 inches by 52 feet, 7 inches. The ferry was powered by Busch-Sulzer direct drive diesel. (Author's collection.)

There was only one like her anywhere in the world, and as one former captain once joked, "one was enough." The streamlined art deco *Kalakala* made her debut in 1935 and became a sensation all over the world. She became famous for her moonlight cruises in the 1930s, as pictured here, and for her teeth-shaking vibration. (Author's collection.)

Built on top of the hull of the burned-out San Francisco ferry, *Peralta*, the *Kalakala*, as photographed here with her shining silver super structure, became an icon of Seattle and the Pacific Northwest by the late 1930s. She sailed mainly on the waters between Bremerton and Seattle. (Author's collection.)

The *Kalakala* became the second-most photographed object in the world, second only to the Eiffel Tower in Paris. She even graced the pages of the January 1938 edition of the prestigious *National Geographic* magazine. While referring to her as a "queer-looking craft," she appeared among such well-known Atlantic liners as the *Rex* and *Queen Mary*. (Author's collection.)

By the 1960s, the *Kalakala* was close to the end of her career. Her limited capacity and high-maintenance engines made her of restricted use to the WSF. At the time of the 1962 World's Fair, which she is advertising on her sides in this photograph, she was still ranked as the number-two attraction, just behind the then brand-new Space Needle. (Author's collection.)

After being gutted and converted to a cannery, the *Kalakala* fell into steady decline in Kodiak, Alaska. Rescued by Peter Bevis and the Kalakala Foundation, she made her way back to Seattle in 1998, only to face an even more uncertain future. Efforts to restore the ferry have met one stumbling block after another, and the foundation eventually filed for bankruptcy. The ferry was sold and hauled up to Neah Bay for a short while, where she managed to damage the Makah Reservation's pier. She now sits in Tacoma, waiting for the funds to return her to her once beautiful state. (Photograph by the author.)

In spite of losing nearly all her original fittings, touches of the *Kalakala*'s past still remain. The graceful wrought-iron and brass art deco staircase on her aft end is still in place, showing a glimmer of what once was. (Photograph by the author.)

Today, the main passenger cabin of the *Kalakala* retains only the curves of her former art deco elegance. Brass frames remain around the windows, but bench seats and polished tile are a mere memory now. The *Kalakala* was constructed on the hull of the *Peralta* at the Lake Washington Shipyards in Seattle in 1935. The hull and superstructure were steel, and she measured 276 feet, 5 inches by 55 feet, 7 inches. The ferry was powered by one 3,000-horsepower, Busch-Sulzer direct-drive diesel. (Photograph by the author.)

The *Crosline*, shown here with only one wheelhouse in the 1930s, originally sailed between Seattle and Manchester, but was sold by Black Ball for use in Vancouver, British Columbia. When the ferry was no longer of use there, she was purchased by the Washington State Highway Department for use on the Tacoma narrows run after the bridge collapsed. In order to bring her back under the U.S. flag, an Act of Congress was required to change the law. She was rebuilt as a double-ended ferry, which prolonged her life for the WSF. (Author's collection.)

The *Crosline* was retired in 1968 and spent a few years on Lake Union before being sold to new owners in the early 1970s. Towed to Coos Bay, Oregon, she was to be turned into a floating restaurant, but was never converted. She was dismantled with parts of her turned into a machine shop, a dock, and a fishing boat. The *Crosline* was built by Marine Construction Company, of Seattle, in 1925. The ferry was made of wood and measured 150 feet, 7 inches by 55 feet, 1 inch. Propulsion was provided by a Cooper-Bessemer diesel engine. (Courtesy of Washington State Ferries.)

The *Leschi* was originally a steam-driven, paddle-wheel ferry on Lake Washington. For Washington State Ferries she filled in at Vashon Island and Mukilteo until 1968. For the rest of her career she was used as a cannery in Alaska, until partially sinking at her mooring outside of Cordova. The hulk was still visible as of 1996, with her upper works completely collapsed. The *Leschi* was constructed in 1913 in Seattle, had a steel hull and wooden superstructure, and measured 169 feet, 11 inches by 50 feet, 3 inches. Originally powered by steam, the power plant was later replaced with a Washington Estep Diesel. (Author's collection.)

The Steel Electric–class vessels once had two other sisters, the *Enetai* and the *Willapa*. Built for the Northwestern Pacific Railroad in 1927, the *Santa Rosa* would later become the *Enetai* on Puget Sound. Here the flank of the boat zips past the photographer in 1927, shortly after she went into service. (Author's collection.)

Captain Peabody needed extra capacity and speed for the booming Bremerton run. The *Enetai*, pictured here shortly after arriving on Puget Sound in 1941, had one wheelhouse removed, her passenger cabin expanded, and her engines replaced with one direct-drive Busch-Sulzer diesel. Her speed increased by nearly four knots and her passenger capacity doubled. (Author's collection.)

The clean sweep of the *Enetai*'s texas deck is evident in this aerial shot taken in the 1940s. Summers would find the upper deck crowded with passengers enjoying the fresh open breezes as the ferry churned her way toward the Bremerton dock. The lack of passengers indicates that, despite the sun, it must be a chilly day on Puget Sound. (Author's collection.)

The WSF did little to alter the *Enetai*'s appearance, although by 1953 when this photograph was taken, they had replaced the large, rectangular windows on the car deck with a neat row of portholes. The larger windows were left from her days in San Francisco and were constantly being broken. The WSF replaced the windows with portholes on the entire class. (Author's collection.)

The WSF retired the *Enetai* in 1967 when the new Super-class ferries arrived. She was sold and returned to San Francisco. Remarkably, the *Enetai* is still in existence today, and is in fine shape, serving as corporate headquarters for Hornblower Yachts under her old name, *Santa Rosa*. (Courtesy of Debbie Lund.)

Hornblower Yachts has attempted to make the ferry look more like her original configuration by adding a wheelhouse to the stern and painting the Southern Pacific ferries logo on her side. The *Santa Rosa* had been beautifully restored as her car deck was finished with a dining room, dance floor, and a full bar for parties and events. (Courtesy of Debbie Lund.)

Looking very much like she did in the 1940s, the *Santa Rosa* still retains her reconfigured cabin. Needed for use during the war years, the trim cabin was sacrificed to give her a carrying capacity of 1,200 passengers. Today, the upper cabin is used as office space. The *Enetai* was constructed in 1927 by General Engineering and Drydock Company, of Alameda, California. The ferry has a steel hull and measures 256 feet by 66 feet. Propulsion was provided by a Busch-Sulzer, direct-drive diesel. (Courtesy of Brandon J. Moser.)

The *Enetai*'s nearly identical sister ferry on the Bremerton route was the *Willapa*, shown here after entering service in 1941. Formerly the *Fresno*, she received the same refurbishment of her passenger cabin and also had her engines replaced with one direct-drive diesel engine. (Author's collection.)

Shown here in about 1954, the ferry looks remarkably the same, save for the portholes and livery. The single-ended configuration kept her on the Seattle-Bremerton route for her entire career. (Author's collection.)

Like the *Enetai*, the *Willapa* returned to San Francisco. Her named returned to *Fresno* and she endured a lay-up that lasted over 30 years. Photographed here in 1994, some of the sporadic work done to restore her is evident. The efforts were not enough to keep the elements at bay. In 2003, she sank at her berth in Richmond. (Courtesy of Brandon J. Moser.)

With her lifeboat discarded on the shore, the former *Willapa* slips into further decay. (Courtesy of Brandon J. Moser.)

Attempts were made to restore the ferry, including replacing her car-deck portholes with windows and the work on the stern pictured here. However, it was her hull that needed the most repair. After three months on the bottom, her hull was patched up with concrete and the ferry was raised. (Courtesy of Brandon J. Moser.)

Where there's water

The Puget Sound area is bountifully blessed with *water*—oceans, lakes, rivers, streams, bays, coves, inlets!

Where there's *Water*, there's breath-taking scenery—pounding surfs, quiet coves, surging streams and gem-like lakes in settings of tall, green timbers.

Where there's *Water*, there's activity—quaint fishing boats, sleek pleasure craft, ocean-going liners and mighty warships.

Where there's *Water*, there's *family fun!* Swimming, fishing, boating, beach-combing or just relaxing after an exciting day around a crackling fire of driftwood.

Get your family together *today*—talk it over; plan to have your share of the fun and varied activities of the Puget Sound Area soon.

WASHINGTON STATE FERRIES

Memories of happier times are seen here as the *Willapa* sails through Rich Passage while a family poses on the deck of the *Enetai* in the 1950s for WSF publicity. Sadly, the *Willapa's* fate seems sealed. Her owners listed the ferry for sale on eBay in the spring of 2005; there were no takers. At last report she was tied up at Mare Island, California, awaiting a buyer. If none can be found, the vessel is going to be sold for scrap. The *Willapa* was built by the Bethlehem Shipping Corporation of San Francisco. Her hull was constructed of steel and she measured 256 feet by 66 feet. Propulsion was provided by a Busch-Sulzer, direct-drive diesel. (Author's collection.)

The *Skansonia* was built in Gig Harbor in 1929 and spent most of her career serving south Vashon Island and the city of Tacoma. For the WSF, she was assigned to the Tahlequah-Point Defiance run, leaving it only when the *Hiyu* replaced her. (Courtesy of Richard Moser.)

Today the *Skansonia* is moored on Lake Union. The car deck is now a banquet hall and can be rented for parties and corporate gatherings. (Courtesy of Richard Moser.)

Featuring beautiful views of Lake Union and the Seattle skyline, the *Skansonia* is a popular place for weddings. For a few years, the *Kalakala* was moored alongside the *Skansonia*—the two old ferries representative of an era long gone on Puget Sound. The *Skansonia*, an all-wood ferry, was built in 1929 by the Skansie Brothers Shipbuilding of Gig Harbor, Washington. She measured 164 feet, 6 inches by 50 feet, 11 inches, and was driven by two Fairbanks-Morse diesel engines. (Courtesy of Brandon J. Moser.)

As the last steam-powered ferry on the West Coast, the SS *San Mateo* was a vessel beloved by all on Puget Sound. With her melodious steam whistle, the ferry was greeted like an old friend by commuters. She sailed first for Black Ball in 1941 and then for Washington State Ferries until Labor Day of 1969. (Courtesy of Washington State Ferries.)

Among the things the *San Mateo* was noted for were her stained-glass clerestory windows, carved columns and mahogany bench seats, and her towering smokestack. After being retired in 1969, she endured a decade of decay and neglect at the Northwest Seaport in Seattle. Shown here shortly before she was sold in 1994 to a Canadian man, she was towed up the Fraser River in British Columbia and moored. (Courtesy of Richard Moser.)

The *San Mateo* is seen here in December 2004. Since moving to Canada in 1994, nothing has been done to preserve the vessel. She is hard aground, routinely flooded by the Fraser River, and slowly falling apart. The vessel next to her is the retired B.C. Ferry, *Queen of Sidney*. (Photograph by the author.)

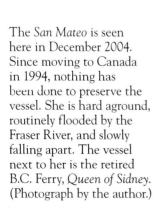

Sadly, pictured is the car deck of the *San Mateo*, showing the six inches of river silt that has built up. Underneath the muck are the thick timbers that once had DeSotos and Studebakers parked on them. Below the decks the *San Mateo*'s engine still remain in place. (Photograph by the author.)

All the glass was removed from the ferry to prevent it from breaking, but nothing was put in to keep the elements out. Aside from the rust along her hull, whole sections of her ceiling have begun to cave in. (Photograph by the author.)

The still waters of the Fraser reflect a sad picture of a once beautiful vessel falling further into decay. Rust riddles her flanks and plants spring out of the woodwork. Still, the trademark WSF green clings to her sides. (Photograph by the author.)

Looking past the empty davit on her port side, the photograph reveals the collapse of her passenger cabin as it starts to peel away from the sides of the boat. Ironically, the *Queen of Sidney* is offering some protection to the ferry, but a heavy winter snowfall will likely cause the collapse of the upper decks. (Courtesy of Brandon J. Moser.)

The stairs to the upper decks are empty and forlorn, host only to "urban explorers" who brave the rotted timbers to get a look at the cabin. Some benches remain, but vandals have knocked over her lunch counter. The vessel is now too far gone to be restored, as her entire superstructure needs to be completely replaced. The *San Mateo* was built in 1922 by Bethlehem Shipbuilding Corporation of San Francisco. She has a steel hull with a wooden superstructure, and measures 230 feet, 4 inches by 63 feet, 8 inches. Propulsion was provided by a triple-expansion steam engine. (Courtesy of Brandon J. Moser.)

The former San Francisco ferry *Golden State*, renamed *Kehloken* by Black Ball, sails into Eagle Harbor in the 1940s. The vessel is all but forgotten by most on Puget Sound. The ferry remains a sad footnote in the history of Bainbridge Island; it was on this ferry that the Japanese residents of the Island were loaded onto for relocation to interment camps for the duration of World War II. (Author's collection.)

The *Kehloken* was assigned to the Seattle-Winslow run for most of her career. Taken here in the later 1940s, this image shows the ferry sailing into Elliott Bay. After larger ferries replaced her, she moved to Vashon Island and Kingston as a relief boat. The early 1970s saw the vessel tied up at the WSF's repair facility in Eagle Harbor, as her all-wood construction was too costly to keep up. (Author's collection.)

Postcards of the *Kehloken* are rare. This one from the 1940s identifies her as a "Bainbridge Island" ferry. She was sold in 1975 to be turned into a floating clubhouse. In 1979 she was set on fire by arsonists while moored on Lake Washington. Charred to the waterline, the hulk was cleaned up and towed out to Possession Point off of Whidbey Island. There she was sunk to be used as an artificial reef. Today, the wreck of the *Kehloken* teems with sea life. The vessel was built in 1926 by General Engineering and Drydock Company of Alameda, California. The ferry was entirely constructed of wood, and measured 239 feet, 8 inches by 60 feet, 3 inches. She was powered by diesel-electric propulsion. (Author's collection.)

Sister to the *Golden State* was the *Golden Age*, renamed *Klahanie* while in service on Puget Sound. Pictured here in the 1940s, she too sailed the Seattle-Winslow run until the increased traffic on the route outpaced her in the early 1950s. The ferry then worked at Kingston-Edmonds and Vashon Island as an extra service boat. (Courtesy of Tom Sanislo.)

Like her other wood-diesel sisters, the *Klahanie* found herself too expensive to repair and of little use to the WSF by the early 1970s. She remained tied up at Eagle Harbor for years until finally purchased in 1975. She was to be towed to California, but never made the trip, ending up in Everett, then moored along the banks of the Duwamish River. (Courtesy of David A. Ruble.)

The *Klahanie* then endured a slow, steady decline. Wedged in the mud of the Duwamish, her all-wood construction began to rot, collapse, and fall apart. The abandoned vessel became home to derelicts and drug addicts seeking shelter. For ten years she remained an eyesore on the river. Photographed here in the summer of 1990, she is just weeks away from her final destruction. (Courtesy of Tom Sanislo.)

In July 1990, she caught fire and burned down to the hull. The charred wreck remained in the same location until 1998 when the hulk was broken up on the spot and hauled away as part of the Duwamish River habitat restoration. The *Klahanie* was constructed in 1927 By General Engineering and Drydock Company of Alameda, California. The ferry was constructed entirely of wood and measured 240 feet, 6 inches by 59 feet, 6 inches. She was powered by diesel-electric propulsion. (Courtesy of Brandon J. Moser.)

The *Golden Poppy* became the *Chetzemoka* on Puget Sound upon her arrival in 1938. For much of her career she worked the Clinton-Mukilteo route, as she is pictured here in the 1940s, becoming the "Chetzie" to her regular customers. (Author's collection.)

Very little about the *Chetzemoka* changed while she was working for the WSF. Shown here in the 1950s, she still looks as she did when working in San Francisco. The *Chetzemoka* continued on Mukilteo-Clinton route for the WSF, though for summers between 1962 and 1965 she did work in the San Juan Islands. (Author's collection.)

Like her sisters, the *Chetzemoka* found herself sidelined after Labor Day of 1973. An aging dinosaur, her low capacity and all-wood construction were strikes against her and she was sold. She was to be given her old name and returned to San Francisco, but while under tow in the spring of 1977 her hull sprung several leaks and she sank off the coast of Washington. The *Chetzemoka* was built in 1927 by General Engineering and Drydock Company of Alameda, California, and measured 239 feet, 11 inches by 60 feet, 3 inches. She was powered by diesel-electric propulsion. (Courtesy of David A. Ruble.)

The M/V *Vashon*, pictured here at Clinton, Whidbey Island, and still sporting the livery of the Kitsap County Transportation Company in 1941, became the last all-wood ferry to sail for the WSF. A complete product of the evergreen state, she was "Washington built" from her keel timbers to her Washington Estep diesel engines. (Author's collection.)

Though originally intended for use on her namesake island, the *Vashon* actually spent more time in the San Juan Islands, where she was nicknamed "Old Reliable." By the 1970s, islanders regarded her as "their" boat, but she did relief work at both Mukilteo and Hood Canal after the bridge sank in 1979. (Courtesy of Tom Sanislo.)

The *Vashon*'s final years put her back in familiar waters in the San Juans. As the new Issaquah-class ferries began to appear in 1979 and 1980, the need for the *Vashon* decreased and her upkeep became increasingly more expensive. (Author's collection.)

Her last sailing was in December 1980. The ferry was tied up for a time at Eagle Harbor before being sold in 1982. For a number of years she lingered at Colman Dock in downtown Seattle, a reminder of the ferry system's simpler days. Pictured here at the dock in late 1981, twilight enfolds the old boat. (Courtesy of Tom Sanislo.)

A group called "Friends of the Vashon" tried to buy the ferry and turn her into a floating restaurant in Friday Harbor, but the group failed to raise the funds. Instead, the *Vashon* was sold again and moved to Port Townsend to be used as a hostel, which only lasted one summer. She was brought up to Alaska in 1986 to be used as a supply boat. Unfortunately, the ferry ran aground outside of Ketchikan and was unable to be towed off. The *Vashon* rolled over on her side, eventually being pulled out by the tide, disappearing from view. She was constructed in 1930 at the Lake Washington Shipyard, of Houghton, Washington, was made entirely of wood, and measured 200 feet by 58 feet. She was powered with a Washington Estep diesel engine. (Courtesy of Tom Sansilo.)

A popular boat in San Diego, the open-deck *Crown City* was less than popular as the *Kulshan* for the WSF. Arriving in 1969, the ferry was sent to help traffic on the Mukilteo-Clinton route, but her lack of a passenger cabin baffled commuters. Greeted with derision from practically the moment she arrived, the *Kulshan* nevertheless sailed for over 10 years. She was scheduled to be retired and sold, but ended up helping out at Hood Canal after the bridge sank. Sold in 1982, she then went to work for the Coast Guard at Governor's Island in New York Harbor. In the 1990s she was sold again and currently works summers under her new name *Governor* on Martha's Vineyard. The *Kulshan* was built in 1954 Moore Drydock Company of Oakland, California. She has a steel hull and measures 242 feet, 5 inches by 65 feet, 1 inch and is powered by diesel-electric propulsion. (Courtesy of Tom Sanislo.)

From Maryland came the M/V *Governor Harry W. Nice* to the rescue in 1954 to add some much-needed carrying capacity to the fleet. Shown here in the 1950s, the ferry was renamed *Olympic*. The state first assigned her to the Lofall-Southpoint run on Hood Canal, and then shifted the ferry to Mukilteo. She would remain there for the next 20 years. (Courtesy of Washington State Ferries.)

The *Olympic* was assigned to the Port Townsend-Keystone run in 1974 and was scheduled to be retired in 1983, but actually continued in service for another 10 years. After the expensive refurbishment of the *Olympic*'s near sister, *Rhododendron*, the state decided to sell the ferry in 1997. (Photograph by the author.)

Today, the ferry sits just across from the ferry dock on Bainbridge Island. Plans to turn her into an excursion boat or museum have never materialized. The *Olympic* falls into further disrepair with each passing year. (Photograph by the author.)

Shadows and rust are the only passengers on the ferry now. Once a familiar profile on countless postcards around Whidbey Island, the *Olympic* is now a sad footnote in the history of the system. (Photograph by the author.)

Snapped in 2003, the *Olympic* looks out of place among the masts of the sail boats in the posh marina. The ferry is fading from history in plain sight. The *Olympic* was built by the Maryland Drydock Company of Baltimore in 1938. The ferry has a steel hull and measures 207 feet, 6 inches by 62 feet. She is powered by a Fairbanks Morse diesel engine. (Photograph by the author.)

The most recent sale was of the passenger-only ferry *Tyee*. The former *Glacier Express* was picked up second-hand by the WSF in 1986, and was put on the Seattle-Bremerton run in hopes of a half-hour commute. Problems with the engines would plague the ferry for her entire career, but it was her wake that caused most of the problems. (Photograph by the author.)

The state's entire passenger-only program was scuttled in 2003, save for the Vashon-Seattle run. The *Tyee* was removed from service almost at once in September of that year and put up for auction on eBay. The ferry sold and was destined for Florida, but was resold before she ever left Puget Sound. Renamed the *Aqua Express*, she now is the sole vessel on a Kingston-Seattle passenger-only route run by a private company. The ferry hasn't proved very successful for her new owners. In the summer of 2005, Aqua Express announced they would be ending service in October 2005. The *Tyee* was built in 1985 by Nichols Brothers of Freeland, Washington. She has an aluminum hull and measures 94 feet, 4 inches by 31 feet, and is powered by diesel propulsion. (Photograph by the author.)

Two

END OF THE
INDEPENDENTS

When the state took over ferry operations in 1951, Alexander Peabody retained a handful of vessels; most notably, the sparkling, streamlined *Chinook*, which had been designed as the "night boat" from Seattle to Victoria. Created by William Francis Gibbs, who designed and built the SS *United States*, the *Chinook* was an elegant vessel that had been an unqualified success for Peabody's Black Ball Line. Also retained was the middle sister between the *Kitsap* and *Vashon*. The M/V *Bainbridge* was similar in appearance to both her sisters and had been a familiar sight to many travelers on Puget Sound. Captain Peabody also kept the *Iroquois*, which he later sold to the subsidiary company Black Ball Transport, the *Malahat*, which was subsequently sold for scrap, and the ferry *Quillayute*, a smaller vessel built for another company in 1923 that had been taken over by Black Ball in the 1930s. Most surprisingly, Peabody kept the then nearly 50-year-old and very outdated *City of Sacramento*. The big steamer had been on the Bremerton run for the last months of World War II, but was moored at Harbor Island for a few years after the war.

Peabody moved what remained of his fleet to British Columbia, building terminals and laying the blueprint for modern ferry operations in the province. When the government bought Captain Peabody out in the early 1960s, it was an amicable sale and Peabody retired. A few of his boats survived well into the 1980s. Under new names, the familiar profiles once on Puget Sound became familiar sights to thousands of British Columbians.

The last independent auto carrier on Puget Sound was not a rival of Captain Peabody. Olympic Ferries Incorporated operated the Port Townsend-Keystone route since the 1940s when Black Ball abandoned the route prior to World War II. Olympic Ferries operated it with a few different vessels, but mainly the *Skansonia*'s near sister, the M/V *Defiance*. By the 1960s, Olympic Ferries experienced increasing traffic, which was a popular tourist route, and were looking to expand operations.

Fortune had it that the Coronado Bridge was opening up in 1969, putting the ferries from the San Diego-Coronado Ferry Company out of a job. The Washington State Ferries snapped up the *Crown City*, later renamed the *Kulshan*. Olympic Ferries bought the M/V *San Diego*, and for a few years it looked as if the operation might work. Running only in the summer months, the ferry system was seldom without customers wanting to cross from Whidbey Island to the picturesque Victorian town of Port Townsend, giving them easy access to the wilds of the Olympic National Park. Regrettably, circumstances dictated otherwise and Olympic Ferries folded. The governor of Washington ordered Washington State Ferries to take over the route, which they did.

The ferry system did not, however, take the two vessels over. Having just rid themselves of nearly all their wooden ferries, they were not about to take on the *Defiance*. It was sold, converted into a dogfish processor, and was last listed on the Coast Guard register as "In service" as of 2000.

The *San Diego* was to be moved to Canada for conversion into a riverboat named *Klondike Queen*, but it never happened. She lingered on the Vancouver waterfront for years. Looking for immediate help in 1979 after the loss of the Hood Canal Bridge, the WSF investigated buying her to use on the canal, but after inspection it would have been too costly to rehabilitate her. She ended up on the Sacramento River until 2000 when she was illegally towed to San Francisco. At last report, the *San Diego*, half converted into a restaurant and partially burned out from an accidental fire, was moored about four miles north of the Antioch Bridge.

Nearly forgotten today, the vessels of Olympic Ferries and the remnants of Captain Peabody's fleet were an important component of travel in both the Puget Sound region and in Canada.

The M/V *Bainbridge* is seen here in service at Horseshoe Bay in the 1950s. The all-wood ferry became a headache for B.C. Ferries. Renamed *Jervis Queen*, her timbers were so soft that women's heels poked through the planking. She was retired in 1966, and spent the next 20 years rotting away on the Fraser River. She sank at her berth in 1986 and broke up on the spot. The *Bainbridge* was built in 1928 by Lake Washington Shipyards of Houghton, Washington. She was entirely made of wood, and measured 177 feet, 7 inches by 55 feet, 2 inches. Propulsion was provided by a Washington Estep diesel. (Author's collection.)

The beautiful *Chinook* cuts like a knife through Puget Sound waters. Her designer, William Gibbs, described her as the "Queen Elizabeth of the Inland Seas." Her debut in 1947 was an immediate success. (Author's collection.)

The full-service dining room was circular, with windows looking out onto Puget Sound. Well over 100 diners could sit and enjoy a meal as the sun set over the Sound as the vessel departed Seattle for Port Angeles. (Author's collection.)

In the lounge, passengers could recline in furnishings provided by Frederick and Nelson, Seattle's premiere department store. The *Chinook* had 100 staterooms, including two bridal suites and accommodations for families. Not tremendously large, the rooms were well fitted and comfortable nonetheless. (Author's collection.)

The wheelhouse of the *Chinook* was the most advanced to grace Puget Sound waters in its era. Advertising the new radar, termed "eyes in the night," Black Ball emphasized the superior safety features of the vessel. (Author's collection.)

Unfortunately it wasn't to last. A mere eight years after her maiden voyage, Captain Peabody removed the *Chinook* from Seattle-Port Angeles-Victoria (British Columbia) service. In 1955, his Canadian fleet needed more capacity, and the *Chinook* was then registered as *Chinook II* in Canada and placed to work on Horseshoe Bay. With her staterooms, formal dining room, and other lounges removed, the vessel suffered a further ignominy by having her bow cut off to allow for front-end loading, spoiling her good looks. (Author's collection.)

Black Ball continued to use the *Chinook* as their flagship. Clear up until the end of operations, brochures and maps still used the old line-drawing of the ferry with her bow, though it had been removed before she went into service in Canada. This 1960 brochure has the drawing with the bow on the front, but the reality of what the vessel looked like was pictured to the left. (Author's collection.)

B.C. Ferries renamed the ferry as the *Sechelt Queen*. She sailed with the "Dogwood Fleet," as it was called, until 1976. She then sailed for the B.C. Highways Department until 1982. Mothballed for a few years, she was dusted off for extra service during the "Expo 86" World's Fair in Vancouver. After being sold back to American interests, she was to be turned into a casino named *Muskegon Clipper* in Alabama in 1996, but there is no record of her after her transfer in 1997. The *Chinook* was built in 1947 by Todd Shipyards of Seattle. She was constructed of steel and measured 318 feet by 65 feet, 5 inches. She was powered by diesel-electric propulsion. (Author's collection.)

This is how the remarkable *City of Sacramento* looked when she came to Puget Sound in 1944. Once the *Asbury Park* in New Jersey, the crack steamer once raced—and beat—the *Kalakala* to Bremerton. Her service on Puget Sound was relatively short, but Captain Peabody had plans for the steamer. (Author's collection.)

Completely unrecognizable, the ferry was stripped to her hull and rebuilt as the *Kahloke* (later the *Langdale Queen*). A beloved ferry to hundreds of Canadians, she was sold in 1977. Later sunk at her berth, she was raised, stripped to her hull and turned into a barge. As of late 2004, the hull, now 101 years old, was still afloat and in use. The *City of Sacramento* was built in by William Cramp and Sons of Philadelphia in 1903. She had a steel hull and measured 308 feet, 4 inches by 57 feet, 5 inches. Her final propulsion was provided by diesel-electric engines. (Author's collection.)

The M/V *Quillayute*, shown here in the 1940s, was a jaunty boat with a large wheelhouse. She had sailed between Edmonds and Kingston and the San Juan Islands before being taken to Canada. B.C. Ferries sold her as rapidly as they could, having had a bevy of mechanical and hull issues. Turned into a fish camp named *Samson IV*, she was reportedly broken up in 2003. The *Quillayute* was built by Winslow Marine Railway & Shipbuilding Company of Winslow, Washington, in 1923. She measured 151 feet, 5 inches by 52 feet and was powered by Washington Estep diesel propulsion. (Author's collection.)

The *Iroquois*, built in 1901, was one of a trio of steamers that came to Puget Sound in 1910. After being sold back to Great Lakes service, Black Ball brought her to the Northwest once again eight years later, completely rebuilt her, and made her the "night ferry" to Victoria. (Author's collection.)

Even with her elegant lady's lounge and stylishly outfitted dining room, the rebuilt steamer looked a bit bulky. Sold to Black Ball Transport in 1952, she was converted into a nearly unrecognizable diesel freighter that sailed until 1969. The *Iroquois* lingered on Lake Union until 1973, when she was sold the Alaska-Shell Corporation for use as a crab processor. After being abandoned, she was taken out to sea and sunk in February 1984. The *Iroquois* was built by Craig Shipbuilding of Toledo, Ohio, in 1901. She was constructed of steel and measured 226 feet, 3 inches by 46 feet. Her final propulsion was powered by a diesel engine. (Author's collection.)

The *Napa Valley* was another San Francisco ferry purchased by Captain Peabody for use on Puget Sound. Shown here sailing on the bay, the ferry had a bumpy career in the Northwest. Upon arrival on Puget Sound, the vessel distinguished itself by catching on fire and burning out the passenger cabin. She was quickly rebuilt, renamed *Malahat*, and put into service. (Author's collection.)

The *Malahat*, pictured here toward the end of her career in the late 1940s, was never considered for Canadian service, even though she had not been included in the sale to the WSF. Captain Peabody sold her for scrap in 1952. After moving to Portland in 1955, the ferry caught fire again, this time destroying the entire vessel. The *Malahat* was built by Union Iron Works in 1910. She was powered by triple-expansion steam propulsion. (Author's collection.)

The *Defiance*, seen here in the 1940s, was a no-frills ferryboat. Built by the same yard as the *Skansonia*, she took her name from Point Defiance, for which she had been originally built to serve. The bulk of her career saw her at Port Townsend, however. The *Defiance* as built by Skansie Brothers Shipbuilding of Gig Harbor, Washington, in 1927. She was constructed entirely of wood, and measured 156 feet, 6 inches by 49 feet, 2 inches. Propulsion was provided by Washington Estep diesel engines. (Author's collection.)

Far from the sunny shores of her former life, the *San Diego* sits rusting along the Vancouver waterfront in the 1980s. In use for only a few brief years for Olympic Ferries, she never saw active service again. The *San Diego* was built in 1931 by the Moore Drydock Company of Oakland, California. She has a steel hull and wooden superstructure. (Author's collection.)

Three

THE CURRENT FLEET

Today's fleet is a dichotomy of old and new. Tethered at one end to the past is the Steel Electric class, those wonderful old San Francisco ferries that first sailed when Calvin Coolidge was president. On the other end is the mammoth Jumbo Mark II class, modern in every sense of the word, and capable of hauling 2,500 passenger and 218 cars.

In between are the Evergreen State–class, the Super-, the Jumbo-, and the Issaquah-class ferries that have become part of the landscape and the subject of hundreds of postcards; their scenic profiles synonymous with Puget Sound and the Pacific Northwest.

The ferries are not static, however. Upgrades above and below decks keep them up to the current level of safety standards. Five boats have been expanded to carry more cars. Most visible are the interior upgrades many of the ferries have received in recent years, bringing them up to more modern tastes and making them far more comfortable than their former utilitarian drabness.

Generations of travelers on Puget Sound have laid claim to "their" ferries. With the Steel Electrics facing retirement, a new generation of boats will make their way onto Puget Sound and take their place among the onshore communities.

Photographs will one day depict the final moments of the "old" Super, Jumbo, and Issaquah class too, replaced by new boats and passing into the Ghost Fleet themselves. Ferries will always be a part of Puget Sound, however, living in photographs, in name, and in the memories of the millions of people who travel on them each year.

The M/V *Illahee* is shown here about 1945. The vessel is, according to the WSF, the oldest operating ferry in the world. Starting out as the *Lake Tahoe*, she nearly sank on her journey up from San Francisco in a fierce storm. Arriving a little worse for wear, she spent the next five years running an astounding 23 hours a day. (Author's collection.)

The WSF first enclosed the large windows, as seen here, within the first months of operation. However, in 1957 and 1958 the four Steel Electrics (*Illahee, Nisqually, Quinault,* and *Klickitat*) were all expanded by eight feet and modernized. It was the first major alteration to their former slim San Francisco profiles. This photograph predates that modernization. Here the *Illahee* still has her wooden deck rails, thus dating the photograph between 1953 and 1957. (Author's collection.)

Completely rebuilt in 1986, the *Illahee* lost her distinctive funnel and wooden superstructure, and, unfortunately, every bit of her classic profile from 1927. After working many years on the Port Townsend–Keystone run, the *Illahee* now is the inter-island boat in the San Juans. (Courtesy of Richard Moser.)

Sailing in to Friday Harbor, the *Illahee* is dwarfed by her sailing companions in the Islands—the Super class *Yakima*, *Elwha*, and *Kaleetan*. Still performing a vital role, the nearly 80-year-old ferry sails strictly between San Juan, Orcas, Shaw, and Lopez Islands, only coming to Anacortes for fueling. (Photograph by the author.)

Looking very much like the old-profile ferry logo, the *Illahee* sails toward the Friday Harbor dock. The vessel will be retired and sold by the end of the decade. The *Illahee* was built in 1927 at Moore Drydock Company of Oakland, California, and measures 256 feet, 2 inches by 73 feet, 10 inches. She is powered by diesel-electric propulsion. (Photograph by the author.)

The M/V *Stockton* is pictured here in the 1930s as she looked on San Francisco Bay before coming north and becoming the *Klickitat*. The six ferries in the Steel Electric class were once identical in nearly every way. (Author's collection.)

The early years of the *Klickitat*'s service had her working between Edmonds, where she is making a landing in this photograph in the 1940s, and between Kingston and Port Ludlow. The WSF shifted the ferry to the San Juan Islands in the early 1950s, where she was to spend much of her career. (Author's collection.)

Like the *Vashon*, the *Klickitat* became an "Island boat," faithfully serving the San Juan, Orcas, Shaw, and Lopez Islands, along with Anacortes and Sidney, British Columbia. Other than paint and portholes, the state did little to change her outward appearance. This photograph also shows the original wooden handrails, dating it between 1953 and 1957. (Author's collection.)

The *Klickitat* was the first Steel Electric to be remodeled in 1982. Unfortunately, the new steel cabin did away with the observation room at either end of the cabin, replacing it with crew quarters and then a shelter deck. The arrangement proved not to be popular and was not used for the other Steel Electrics. (Courtesy of Richard Moser.)

After a short stint of service back in the San Juan Islands, the practically new *Klickitat* took over at Port Townsend–Keystone in the early 1980s and she has remained there ever since. Her long sweeping promenade deck is a popular place to be during summer crossings. (Photograph by the author.)

Deemed unnecessary on a ferry the size of the Steel Electrics, the shelter deck option was eliminated from the other three vessels. This area present on the *Klickitat* forever sets her apart from others in the class. (Photograph by the author.)

During the summer months, the *Klickitat* is packed to capacity with vessels heading toward the wilds of the Olympic Peninsula. Once rated at 75 cars, with the addition of upgraded safety equipment capacity is now around 64. The *Klickitat* was built by the Bethlehem Shipping Corporation of San Francisco, California and measures, 256 feet by 73 feet, 10 inches. She has a steel hull and is powered by diesel-electric propulsion. (Photograph by the author.)

The *Redwood Empire* would spend just 14 years under that name before becoming the *Quinault* on Puget Sound for over the next 60 years. Shown here in the 1930s, the ferry would soon be out of a job on San Francisco Bay. (Author's collection.)

The *Quinault*, shown here in the 1950s, spent much of her career at Vashon Island—over 30 years. When scheduled for rebuilding in the 1980s, a small but vocal faction from the island lobbied to keep the ferry "as is" as a historical landmark. Unfortunately, the expense of keeping the very active vessel with her original wood cabin was not economically practical. (Author's collection.)

Models pose as passengers in this early publicity shot taken aboard a Steel Electric for the Washington State Ferries. The captain points out some interesting landmark to a group of passengers who seem just a little too happy for the occasion. (Author's collection.)

The *Quinault* became immortalized on film in the 2002 thriller *The Ring*. Some slight Hollywood modifications were made to the ferry for dramatic purposes, but the scene, which involves an out-of-control horse on the car deck, is one of the most memorable of the film. (Photograph by the author.)

In the twilight of her career, the *Quinault*, or "Q-boat" as she is affectionately called by the WSF employees, spends most of her time filling in for the other Steel Electrics and the *Rhododendron* during their maintenance cycles. (Courtesy of Khristopher LaPlante.)

Certain elements of the old cabin were built into the *Quinault*, though the hominess of the wood cabin couldn't be entirely replicated. Still, the archways into the forward observation room and the oak trim and frosted glass of the galley made for some elegant touches, harkening back to the ferry's days on San Francisco Bay. The *Quinault* was built by Moore Drydock Company of Oakland, California, in 1927 and measures 256 feet by 73 feet, 10 inches. She is powered by diesel-electric propulsion. (Courtesy of Indra S. Black.)

The last boat of the quartet is the *Nisqually*. Formerly the *Mendocino* on San Francisco Bay, the ferry spent much of her early career working the Edmonds-Kingston–Port Ludlow run before shifting up to the San Juans. Here she is pictured at the ferry dock in Anacortes in the 1940s. (Author's collection.)

The *Nisqually* continued to serve the same basic routes for the WSF. Like the others in the class, she underwent some minor cosmetic changes in the early years of state ownership before the major renovations in 1958. (Author's collection.)

With her wooden superstructure evident in this photograph, the *Nisqually* would often spend summers in the San Juans throughout the 1970s and 1980s. (Courtesy of David A Ruble.)

Remodeled in the same fashion as the *Quinault* and the *Illahee*, the *Nisqually* went back to work at Kingston for a time until traffic outpaced her. From the late 1980s the ferry worked as relief and back up, ending her career as the inter-island ferry in the San Juans. (Courtesy of Richard Moser.)

With no more coffee to be served, no more doughnuts to be eaten, no more popcorn to toss to seagulls on a sunny crossing, the galley of the *Nisqually* is now filled with shadows. Empty ferryboats are somewhat unsettling as they are meant to be filled with people, the air laden with conversation. Today, the *Nisqually* presents a lonely countenance. (Courtesy of Brandon J. Moser.)

Today, the *Nisqually* is tied up in Eagle Harbor. Officially retired, the ferry last sailed in 2003 and will likely never see active service again. The *Nisqually* was built by the Bethlehem Shipping Corporation of San Francisco and measures 256 feet by 73 feet, 10 inches. Its power is provided by diesel electric propulsion. (Photograph by the author.)

The former Maryland ferry *Governor Herbert R. O'Conor* arrived on Puget Sound in 1953 to become the *Rhododendron* for the WSF. First assigned to service on Hood Canal, she later became a mainstay on the Mukilteo-Clinton run. Shown here in the 1950s, the "Rhody" appears to be in Elliott Bay. (Author's collection.)

After working the Mukilteo run, the "Rhody" moved over to the Port Townsend–Keystone run. In the early 1980s, she was mothballed in Eagle Harbor for nearly a decade. Shown here during her lay up, the ferry was pulled into the yard to be refurbished in the 1990. (Courtesy of Richard Moser.)

Refurbishing the "Rhody" became an embarrassment for the state when the cost jumped several million over budget. The *Rhododendron* was far more weathered than first thought. The entire passenger cabin had to be reconstructed with new steel. She came out of the yard with very little original steel left in her. (Photograph by the author.)

The *Rhododendron* is small enough to be pulled completely onto land for hull work. Shown here at Dakota Creek Shipyard in Anacortes, the ferry is having annual maintenance done. After her yearly yard period, the "Rhody" goes back to her normal route, Point Defiance–Tahlequah run. The *Rhododendron* was built by Maryland Drydock Company of Baltimore in 1947. She measures 227 feet, 6 inches by 62 feet and is powered by diesel propulsion. (Courtesy of Brandon J. Moser.)

The first lady of Washington State Ferries sails on her sea trials in 1954. The *Evergreen State* was the first ferry built for the new system. At the time, she was the largest, most modern ferry afloat. (Author's collection.)

The name of the ferry is an anomaly in the system. As originally planned, the trio was to be *Evergreen State*, *Vacation State*, and *Washington State*. The latter two names sparked a public outcry among historians and commuters alike and were thus dropped to become *Klahowya* and *Tillikum*. (Courtesy of Brandon J. Moser.)

Initially assigned to the Seattle-Winslow (Bainbridge Island) run in 1954, the *Evergreen State* was reassigned to the San Juan Islands in 1959. There she settled in and became a "San Juan" boat, seldom leaving the run over the next 40 years. Here she is sailing toward the Anacortes dock in the summer of 1998, though the photograph could have been snapped anytime between 1959 and 2000. (Photograph by the author.)

Puget Sound cruises
on the most scenic bridges in Washington State

For years, the Evergreen State–class ferries were used for promotional purposes by the WSF. Up until 1967, when the *Hyak* appeared, the stylized renderings of the *Evergreen State* or her near sisters appeared on maps, brochures, and even billboards. (Author's collection.)

Only rarely did the *Evergreen State* leave the San Juans, but one summer in 2000 she was the only boat available to work on the Bremerton run when the *Walla Walla* unexpectedly broke down. Shown here at the new Bremerton dock, the ferry was a welcome sight to many stranded commuters. (Photograph by the author.)

The *Evergreen State*'s central mast, which contains her lighting for making the international run to Canada, set her apart from her nearly identical sisters. Once the primary international ferry, the *Evergreen State* no longer makes the run to Sidney, British Columbia. (Courtesy of Brandon J. Moser.)

May 2003 saw the last run of the *Evergreen State* to Sidney. The Issaquah-class ferry *Chelan* has been SOLAS (Safety Of Life At Sea) upgraded as required for the international run to take the *Evergreen State*'s place. (Courtesy of Brandon J. Moser.)

In October 2004, the *Evergreen State* turned 50. For those years of outstanding service, she received the traditional gold bands around her funnels. She has been placed in mothballs, however, and is used only when there is no other boat available. The *Evergreen State* is one of three Evergreen State–class vessels that includes the *Tillikum* and *Klahowya*. Puget Sound Bridge and Drydock Company of Seattle built the vessels in 1954, 1958, and 1959. They measure 310 feet by 73 feet and are powered by diesel-electric propulsion. (Courtesy of Brandon J. Moser.)

The second ferry in the Evergreen State class, the *Klahowya*, arrived at Vashon Island in 1958 and, with only a few exceptions, has been there ever since. Shown here at the Vashon dock early in her career, the ferry has had a remarkable 47-year run on the same route. The *Klahowya* has had two major refurbishments, but is in every sense a "Vashon" ferry. (Author's collection.)

Shown here is the refurbished interior of the *Klahowya*, displaying modern airline-style seats. One of the biggest improvements made to the interior of the vessel was the lighting, which had previously been somewhat insufficient. The new interior is much brighter, finished out in blue, tan, and light brown. (Courtesy of Brandon J Moser.)

Ferries look very odd when out of their element. Dry-docking is another necessity for vessels that spend their lives in salt water. Elevated in dry-dock at Dakota Creek Shipyard in Anacortes, the *Klahowya* receives a fresh scraping from marine growth and a new coat of paint. Ferries provide jobs from deck hands to yard workers all up and down the Sound. (Photograph by the author.)

The *Klahowya* approaches the Vashon Island dock, a sight familiar to residents for literally a generation. Sailing toward Fauntleroy in West Seattle is her nearly identical sister, the *Tillikum*. (Courtesy of Brandon J. Moser.)

Her name meaning "greetings" in Chinook jargon, the *Klahowya* presents a stunning view for a photograph on a sunny Puget Sound day. Her future may have her assigned to the southern end of Vashon Island, working between Point Defiance and Tahlequah, but hopefully she will remain a "Vashon ferry" her entire career. (Courtesy John S. Kwant, Kwant and Mairs Graphics, Lynnwood, Washington.)

Last of the trio of Evergreen State–class vessels is the *Tillikum*, shown here just after completion in 1959. Her name meaning "friends," in Chinook, she first went into service between Seattle and Winslow, replacing the *Evergreen State*. (Author's collection.)

After being bumped by the *Elwha* in 1968, the *Tillikum* roved around the Sound. She has worked long stretches at Kingston, Edmonds, Vashon Island, and even up in the San Juan Islands. For the last decade or so she has settled in at Vashon Island. (Courtesy of Washington State Ferries.)

Before being refurbished in 1994, the *Tillikum* didn't have a name board under her wheelhouse windows, but had the name painted directly onto the steel in green. Along with new, wider wheelhouse windows, the ferry also received a name board like the rest of the ferries in the fleet. (Courtesy of Richard Moser.)

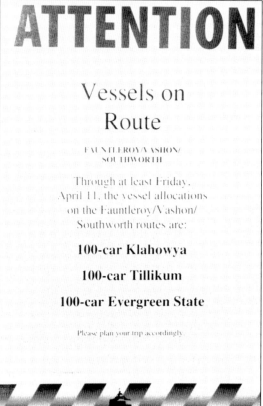

ATTENTION

Vessels on Route

FAUNTLEROY/VASHON/
SOUTHWORTH

Through at least Friday,
April 11, the vessel allocations
on the Fauntleroy/Vashon/
Southworth routes are:

100-car Klahowya

100-car Tillikum

100-car Evergreen State

Please plan your trip accordingly.

For a rare few weeks in 2003, all three Evergreen State–class ferries worked at Vashon Island. Akin to rare planet alignments, it is not very often that all the ferries in a class work one route at the same time. Pairings occur frequently, but to see all members of one class working together is unique. (Courtesy of Brandon J. Moser.)

A warm October sun bathes the *Tillikum* as she approaches the Fauntleroy dock. Lincoln Park, adjacent to the ferry dock, provides a beautiful backdrop to do some ferry watching. (Photograph by the author.)

Replacing the elderly, all-wood *Skansonia* on the Point Defiance–Tahlequah run in 1967 was the *Hiyu*. Built specially for the route, the tiny ferry, whose name means "plenty," was a welcome sight to truck drivers who now had ample room to get their trucks across Dalco Passage. This photograph was snapped by the author's father just a few months after the *Hiyu* went into service for the first time in 1967. (Courtesy of James R. Pickens.)

Lunchtime on the *Hiyu* consists of one coffee vending machine. So tiny was the vessel that only the one machine could be shoehorned into the cabin. She was eventually outpaced by traffic on the Point Defiance run and the WSF shifted her up to the San Juans for inter-island service. (Courtesy of Brandon J. Moser.)

The *Hiyu*, which at night looked like some sort of odd, water-traveling UFO, became a welcome sight to commuters in the San Juans. The ferry rarely broke down, going over two years without missing a run. (Photograph courtesy of Richard Moser.)

The *Hiyu*'s slow speed and ever-shrinking capacity even made her of little use in the San Juans. She was replaced by a Steel Electric as the inter-island ferry and was thus moved to Eagle Harbor. (Courtesy of Brandon J. Moser.)

Unused for a number of years, the ferry is now officially retired from active service. The tiny boat is used now mainly as a training platform for new hires to the WSF. The *Hiyu* was built by Gunderson Brothers Engineering Company of Portland, Oregon, in 1967, and measures 162 feet by 63 feet, 1 inch. She is powered by diesel propulsion. (Courtesy of Brandon J Moser.)

Washington State Ferries
Scenic Guide and Map

Puget Sound

OLYMPIC PENINSULA · HURRICANE RIDGE · HOOD CANAL
KITSAP PENINSULA · VASHON ISLAND · WHIDBEY ISLAND
BAINBRIDGE ISLAND · LOPEZ ISLAND · SAN JUAN ISLAND
SHAW ISLAND · ORCAS ISLAND · VANCOUVER ISLAND

Shown here in 1967 with her green paint stripe too high is the *Hyak*, the first of the Super class ferry that was designed to modernize the fleet and retire a multitude of old, inefficient boats. The proportions of the vessel, nearly 400 feet in length and with a carrying capacity of 160 cars and 2,500 passengers, was unlike anything seen on Puget Sound to date. (Courtesy of James R. Pickens.)

The *Hyak* became the new darling of WSF publicity, appearing on maps and brochures put out all over the country. Assigned to the Seattle-Bremerton run, she retired the *Willapa* and the *Kalakala*. (Author's collection.)

A gray day in Seattle shows an almost-new *Hyak* tied up at Colman Dock, with the solemn spire of the Smith Tower rising in the background. At a speed of 20 knots, the *Hyak* cut the commute time to Bremerton down to about 45 minutes, making her name, which means "fast or speedy," apt. (Courtesy of David A Ruble.)

After 13 years on the Bremerton run, a drop off in traffic on the route sent the *Hyak* northward to Kingston-Edmonds. A particularly low tide in summer of 1988 makes it look as if the ferry is about to run aground in Edmonds. (Courtesy of Richard Moser.)

W. C. Nickum and Sons' incredibly versatile design of Super class made them ideal for many routes, including the San Juan Islands. Summers often found the *Hyak* leaving from Anacortes, as seen here, to the San Juan Islands, where her large capacity and low wake won over many fans. (Photograph by the author.)

After an absence of nearly 20 years, the *Hyak* was regularly assigned to the Bremerton run again. The passenger cabin on the Super class is split into two levels, with the galley upstairs surrounded by a long promenade deck. Drenched in the July sunshine, the *Hyak* is about to depart for Bremerton. (Photograph by the author.)

While the other ferries in the class have all been refurbished, repeal of the motor vehicle excise tax cut funds off for the *Hyak* to be rebuilt. Her interior today remains nearly exactly as it did in 1967—utilitarian in every sense of the word. The ferry is scheduled to be retired by the end of the decade. The *Hyak*, *Kaleetan*, *Yakima*, and *Elwha* are Super-class ferries built by National Steel & Shipbuilding Company of San Diego in 1967 and 1968. They measure 382 feet, 2 inches by 73 feet, 2 inches and are powered by diesel-electric propulsion. (Courtesy of Indra S. Black.)

Her name meaning "arrow," the *Kaleetan* cuts through the waters of the San Juans Islands. Originally assigned to the Seattle-Winslow run, she was displaced by the *Spokane* and moved north in 1973, where she has been more or less ever since. (Courtesy of Brandon J. Moser.)

Completely rebuilt in 1999, the *Kaleetan* now looks like a brand new ferry. Her interior was completely refurbished and modernized, with coastal Native American artwork decorating the walls, and she looks nothing like the former stark, utilitarian boat she once was. Shown here is the number-two, lower-end passenger cabin. The ferry now spends winters on the Seattle-Bremerton run and summers in the San Juans. (Photograph by the author.)

Morning light falls on the *Kaleetan*'s massive funnel as the ferry prepares for an early-morning departure from Anacortes. (Photograph by the author.)

The aft-end shelter deck of the *Kaleetan* frames the masts and sails of the boats moored in Friday Harbor, San Juan Island. The partially enclosed area of the promenade deck is appropriately named, providing shelter from wind and rain. Riders have been enjoying this view for over 30 years in the San Juans. (Photograph by the author.)

The beauty of the San Juans is framed by a window along the car deck. While the setting may be the same day in and day out, the ever-changing conditions on Puget Sound make each day starkly different from the one that preceded it. (Photograph by the author.)

Completely rebuilt in 1999, the *Kaleetan*'s rows of square wheelhouse windows were replaced by the larger ones seen here. However, the middle window proved to be bothersome when its odd, narrow contours made it difficult to see through. It was replaced a few years later by a much wider window, correcting the problem. (Photograph by the author.)

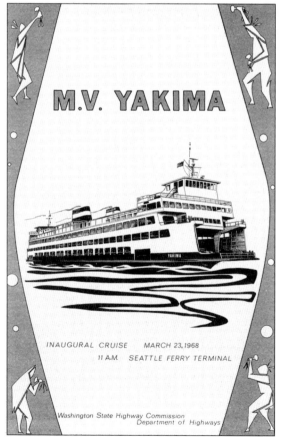

M.V. YAKIMA

INAUGURAL CRUISE   MARCH 23, 1968
11 A.M.   SEATTLE FERRY TERMINAL

Washington State Highway Commission
Department of Highways

Third in the class was the *Yakima*. For each new vessel, the WSF printed a commemorative booklet, detailing the specifics of the vessels, the launch, and what ferries it would replace. The Yakima's booklet was particularly artistic. (Author's collection.)

By the late 1980s and through the 1990s, the *Yakima* became a familiar sight on the Kingston-Edmonds run. Shown here in the late 1980s, the ferry was still a few years from being outpaced by traffic, but that situation was soon to change. (Courtesy of Richard Moser.)

Framed by boats at Kingston, the *Yakima* dominates the horizon. (Photograph by the author.)

The *Yakima* was refurbished in the winter of 1999–2000, and emerged with arguably the most handsome interior of the quartet. Shown here is the galley, which is finished in dark blue, brown, and tan. (Courtesy of Brandon J. Moser.)

Displaced by the new *Puyallup* and the Jumbo ferry *Spokane*, the *Yakima* is now a year-round resident of the San Juans. A multi-million dollar rebuilding by Todd Shipyard has made the *Yakima* a virtually new vessel. Here she is pulling into the Anacortes dock in July 2005 while Mount Baker hides in the clouds. (Photograph by the author.)

With afternoon sailings sold out, the *Yakima* approaches the Anacortes dock in the summer of 2005. Every one of the 160 spaces for cars will be utilized on this trip. (Photograph by the author.)

Joining the fleet in 1968, the *Elwha* was undergoing a major upgrade in December 1990 when a winter storm hit, with 80 mile per hour winds and snow. Known as the "Artic Express," it slammed through the Puget Sound region. Snapping her mooring lines, the *Elwha* bashed into the pier, demolishing much of it and causing the major damage to the boat seen here. (Courtesy of Richard Moser.)

A closer shot reveals the extent of some of the damage. According to a state official, the car deck looked similar to a piece of crumpled tin foil. The unexpected damage delayed the refurbishment and added a substantial amount of cost to the project. (Courtesy of Richard Moser.)

With the damage repaired, the *Elwha*, in addition to being the first Super class to be retrofitted with an elevator, was SOLAS upgraded for sailing between Anacortes to Sidney, British Columbia. Having just made a sharp turn, the *Elwha* leans to port briefly before righting herself. (Photograph by the author.)

Instantly recognizable by the squares cut into her sides for the additional life rafts, the *Elwha* approaches Anacortes having sailed directly from Sidney, British Columbia, in July 2005. On board, walk-on passengers have gathered at the front of the boat to disembark via the overhead walkway for inspection by United States Customs. (Photograph by the author.)

The *Elwha* was the first to be refurbished in 1990–1991. Her interior received a "refurbish lite" compared to the *Yakima* and *Kaleetan*. New tile, upholstery, and artwork were about the only flourishes the *Elwha* got. Despite this, she still looks far less utilitarian than the *Hyak*. (Photograph by the author.)

Just five short years after the Super class arrived, two new and much larger ferries arrived that were part of the Jumbo class. At 440 feet long and with a capacity of 206 cars, the ferries were then the largest double-ended vessels in the world. First to arrive was the *Spokane*, seen here approaching the dock in Winslow, Bainbridge Island. (Courtesy of Richard Moser.)

Designed by Philip Spaulding, there were to have been four of the Jumbos, but only the *Spokane* and *Walla Walla* were built. The *Spokane* became a familiar sight to residents of Bainbridge Island, staying on the route from 1972 until 1999. (Courtesy of Richard Moser.)

A product of the early 1970s, the *Spokane* was fitted out with orange, yellow, and gold. Her refurbished interior now includes blue, black, and purple. She has also been retrofitted with an elevator, shown in the photograph. Her cacophony of color, which was used as a test for materials for the Jumbo Mark II class, earned her the nickname of the "clown boat." (Courtesy of Indra S. Black.)

With the Olympic Mountains providing a dramatic backdrop, the *Spokane* sails toward the Kingston dock. The ferry's sleek profile makes her look lower in the water than she actually is. The *Spokane* and *Walla Walla* both became the new icons of the Seattle area, appearing in countless postcards, photographs, and movies. (Photograph by the author.)

A delight for passengers, particularly children, is the large relief map of the Puget Sound basin. The only original interior feature left on board after the refurbishment, the map is a focal point on the vessel. The *Spokane* and *Walla Walla* are the Jumbo class ferries and were built by Todd Shipyards of Seattle in 1972. They measure 440 feet by 87 feet and are powered by diesel-electric propulsion. (Courtesy of Indra S. Black.)

Identical in every way, the *Walla Walla* spent a season in the San Juans before legalities over the mass-transportation funds used in her construction brought her back to the Seattle-Bainbridge run. Problems with her wake had made her impractical for use in the narrow passages of the islands as well. (Courtesy of Richard Moser.)

Since the Jumbo Mark II's have been added to the fleet, the *Walla Walla*, which like the *Spokane* had spent all her time between Seattle and Bainbridge Island, began to wander. Often she can now be found filling in for her sister at Kingston-Edmonds, or taking over for the *Hyak* on the Bremerton run. (Photograph by the author.)

Dawn backlights the smartly designed funnel on the *Walla Walla* before she departs Bremerton for Seattle. The gumdrop-shaped funnel designed by Phillip Spaulding blends perfectly with the long lines of the ferry. (Photograph by the author.)

The dual whistles of the Jumbos are the most harmonious on Puget Sound since perhaps the steam whistle of the *San Mateo*. As a B-flat major fifth tone, the horns can be heard for miles in every direction. (Photograph by the author.)

The otherwise fine vessels were cursed with the most uncomfortable seats to ever be placed in a ferry. The "tea cups" were bolted to the floor and arranged in such a way as to make it impossible to carry on a conversation with a fellow passenger sitting right next to you. Already removed from the *Spokane*, in the summer of 2005 the *Walla Walla* shed hers as well, with a full interior refurbishment and the addition of an elevator. (Photograph by the author.)

Known of their dependability, the Jumbos have been two of the most successful ferries in the fleet. So well suited to the central Puget Sound runs were the ferries that plans for the new class of ferries built between 1997 and 1999 were drawn off them. (Photograph by the author.)

No other class of ferries has caused as much controversy as the Issaquah class. From the debut of the first ferry, it was apparent that construction had not been up to standards and the computer system used for the propulsion units was schizophrenic. Here the *Issaquah* is shown here in her original 100-car configuration. (Courtesy of Richard Moser.)

The Issaquah class would unexpectedly pull away from docks or crash into them. Lawsuits were filed and all the vessels were rebuilt. After initial problems of the early years of service, the bugs were ironed out. A second car deck was added, bumping capacity up to 130 cars. The *Issaquah*, *Kittitas*, *Kitsap*, *Cathlamet*, *Chelan*, and the *Sealth* are Issaquah-class ferries. They were all built by Marine Power & Equipment of Seattle between 1979 and 1982. They measure 328 feet by 78 feet, 8 inches, and power is provided by diesel propulsion. (Photograph by the author.)

Second out of the yard at Marine Power & Equipment was the *Kittitas*. Of the six boats that would be built, the "Kit," as she is known, has been the most trouble-free. After a few months here and there in the San Juans, the ferry has been regularly assigned to the Mukilteo-Clinton run since 1981. (Courtesy of Richard Moser.)

Framed by the Mukilteo dock, the *Kittitas* departs for Clinton on Whidbey Island. Like the *Issaquah*, she would be rebuilt in 1990 with a mezzanine to carry additional cars. (Courtesy of Richard Moser.)

Here the original main passenger cabin of the *Kittitas* is seen. Crews on the Mukilteo run have kept the ferry spotless, but nothing could be done about the bland, no-frills interiors of the Issaquah-class boats. In the last few years, each boat has gone into the yard to be gutted and have had a new interior put in. The *Kittitas* received her new interior in 2003. (Photograph by the author.)

This is the *Kittitas* as she looks today, with seagulls soaring overhead. Even with the additional car deck, it is easy to spot why the ferries were originally dubbed the "new Evergreen State class." (Photograph by the author.)

Functional, but always a bright spot on deck, the life rings are beacons of bright orange-red against the green of the deck railing. The vivid color is, of course, designed to be more easily spotted on the water. (Photograph by the author.)

Light, color, and shadow are elements that are always changing on the waters of Puget Sound. While nearly always calm in the summer, even the inland seas can turn fierce in the fall and winter. A break in an autumn storm lights the *Kittitas* with moody shadows as the ferry sails toward Clinton. (Photograph by the author.)

Billowing clouds, threatening wind, and rain dwarf the *Kittitas* as she makes another safe and successful trip to Mukilteo. Sixty years earlier, the run was served by vessels made entirely of wood, but the method of transportation has not changed. (Photograph by the author.)

The *Kitsap*, the third of the sextet, joined the fleet in 1980. She began work at Bremerton, Vashon Island, and Mukilteo before settling down as a regular boat on the Bremerton run. She is shown here in the original 100-car configuration approaching the Mukilteo dock. (Courtesy of Richard Moser.)

Rebuilt in 1992 to accommodate 130 cars, the ferry didn't receive an interior renovation until 2000. Used as a relief boat, the *Kitsap* can be found working a multitude of routes while another Issaquah-class ferry is in the yard. (Photograph by the author.)

The port-side, upper-car ramp on the *Kitsap* is deserted on this mid-day crossing from Seattle to Bremerton. Commuter hours and the summer season will find the ferry packed to capacity. (Photograph by the author.)

Though not the largest of the ferries in the fleet, the Issaquah-class vessels are still large boats, particularly when seen from the water. The *Kitsap* is pulling out from the Bremerton dock, loaded with Seahawks fans in the autumn of 2000. (Photograph by the author.)

Arriving in 1981, the *Cathlamet* became infamous for ramming the Mukilteo and Clinton docks within the span of a few days. Having her propulsion systems changed twice, the ferry is now reliable and a regular at Mukilteo. (Courtesy of Richard Moser.)

Since joining the fleet in 1981, the *Cathlamet* and the *Kittitas*, pictured here, have seldom been apart. (Courtesy of Richard Moser.)

Rebuilt in 1993 and with an interior upgrade in 2001, the *Cathlamet* is basically a new ferry. Like the others in the class, her original wheelhouse windows have been replaced with wider, longer panes to aid in visibility. (Photograph by the author.)

Ferries have become part of the scenery in Washington, like the mountains and forests. Here, *Cathlamet* departs Mukilteo for Clinton with a fisherman taking scant notice of the vessel as she slowly moves out for Whidbey Island before increasing to full speed. (Photograph by the author.)

A puff of diesel melds into the twilight as the *Cathlamet*'s engines begin to push her forward. The WSF has made a conscious effort to reduce emissions by ferries, and it is rare to see any vessels' smoke other than when powering up to first leave the dock, as is the case here. (Photograph by the author.)

Recognizing her status as a "Mukilteo boat," the *Cathlamet* has the wheel and navigation equipment from the *Olympic* on display in her passenger cabin. The *Olympic* had been on the run for 20 years; the *Cathlamet* has already broken that record. (Photograph by the author.)

The difference in profiles here is the difference in 50 years of maritime design. The *Quinault* sails toward Edmonds while the *Chelan* is bound for Kingston. Once a regular on the Kingston run, the *Chelan* has been displaced by much bigger boats. (Courtesy of Richard Moser.)

Once the Supers were moved to the Kingston-Edmonds run, the 100-car *Chelan*, built in 1981, moved to the San Juans and over to the Bremerton run. (Courtesy of Brandon J. Moser.)

The *Chelan* became the last Issaquah-class ferry to be rebuilt with the additional car deck. After returning to service for a few years, the ferry went into Everett Shipyards to be SOLAS upgraded and have her interior refurbished. (Courtesy of Brandon J. Moser.)

Laden with Mariners' fans, the newly expanded *Chelan* leaves the Bremerton dock in May 2000. The huge crane from the Puget Sound Naval Shipyard has been a backdrop for ferry photographs of Bremerton for decades. (Photograph by the author.)

With her SOLAS upgrades nearly complete, the Chelan sails through the San Juan Islands in the summer of 2005. She is not scheduled to make her first run to Sidney, British Columbia, until the fall of 2006. Until then, the *Elwha* will carry on with the route. (Photograph by the author.)

Sunlight sparkling like diamonds, the M/V *Sealth*, last of the Issaquah class, approaches Rich Passage on the southern end of Bainbridge Island. Completed in 1982, litigation with her builders kept her out of service for nearly two years. (Photograph by the author.)

The *Sealth* has not been converted to carry 130 cars. Still in her original 100-car configuration, the extra deck clearance in her side tunnels has proven to be highly useful in carrying trucks to the San Juans in the winter months. (Photograph by the author.)

This is the port-side tunnel on the *Sealth*. Compare this photograph to the *Kitsap*'s upper ramp on page 109 and note the difference in height. The ferry is likely to remain a 100-car boat, forever setting her apart from her sisters. (Courtesy of Brandon J. Moser.)

This is part of the ferry few ever see—the propeller. The massive four-blade prop of the *Sealth* is in the Dakota Creek Shipyard dry-dock while the vessel undergoes annual maintenance. In addition to hull painting, the propeller is scraped clean of marine growth. (Photograph by the author.)

Looming in dry-dock, the true size of the *Sealth* is evident. Since coming to the San Juans she has had a few unfortunate mishaps, including two groundings, but has otherwise had a fairly uneventful career. (Photograph by the author.)

M/V *Skagit*, one of two identical mono-hulled passenger-only boats, was added to the fleet in 1990. Designed for fast service to Bremerton, the ferry's wallowing in the waves made her extremely unpopular with commuters. The monstrous wake cast off by her hull necessitated the ferry be slowed down, thus dooming a faster commute. The *Skagit* and *Kalama* were built in New Orleans by Equitable-Halter in 1989. They measure 112 feet by 25 feet and are powered by diesel propulsion. (Photograph by the author.)

The *Kalama*, sister to the *Skagit*, is shown here during one of her numerous breakdowns in 1999. The two boats have been the most unreliable in the fleet. Currently, they are assigned to passenger-only service from Vashon Island to downtown Seattle. (Photograph by the author.)

Looking like a toy boat among the skyscrapers of Seattle, the *Kalama* awaits to be called in for duty. When all six passenger-only boats were in operation, the *Kalama* was moored in Seattle in case one of the other boats broke down and a quick stand-in was needed. (Photograph by the author.)

The first new auto ferry built in nearly 20 years for the WSF, the *Tacoma* is shown undergoing sea trials in 1997. The mammoth ferry was designed to alleviate the building traffic at Bainbridge Island and Kingston. (Courtesy of Brandon J. Moser.)

Pictured are the open-house festivities on the *Tacoma* in the fall of 1997 before she went into service. New ferries always spark the public's interest and all the local media greeted the *Tacoma*. In front of the speaker is a model of the *Tacoma*'s namesake, the SS *Tacoma* of 1913. The crack Black Ball steamer was at one time the fastest single-propeller boat in the world, accomplishing 20 knots. The *Tacoma* of today cruises at 18 knots with a maximum speed of 25 knots. (Courtesy of Brandon J. Moser.)

This interior view of the *Tacoma* shows off her comfortable seats in the main passenger cabin. This style of seat would become the fleet standard, replacing the highly uncomfortable chairs of the old Issaquah and Super-class ferries. (Photograph by the author.)

The profile of the *Tacoma* reveals just how closely she was modeled off her predecessors, the Jumbo class. The new giants were given the moniker "Jumbo Mark II" to indicate they were the second generation of a similar class. (Photograph by the author.)

Almost looking like a crystal growth coming from the *Tacoma*'s stack, the Bank of America Tower and Key Tower loom above the ferry as she takes on passengers and cars bound for Bainbridge Island. Somewhat disappointing in looks, the squat, square funnel lacks the simplicity of the one on the Jumbo class. It's the only disappointing feature of an otherwise outstanding class of ferries. (Photograph by the author.)

With the fireboat *Chief Seattle* firing her water cannons behind her, the *Tacoma* blasts her massive whistles indicating her arrival at Colman Dock. Flags fluttering, the ferry is "dressed" for Maritime Week. The traditional landing signal, one long blast followed by two shorts, has been echoing over Seattle for a century. The *Tacoma, Wenatchee,* and *Puyallup* are Jumbo Mark II ferries, built by Todd Shipyards of Seattle in 1997, 1998, and 1999. They measure 460 feet, 2 inches by 90 feet and are powered by diesel-electric propulsion. (Photograph by the author.)

M/V *Wenatchee,* the second of the class, sails under the watchful profile of Mount Rainier. Unlike the Jumbo class, the Mark II's have a passenger cabin on the upper deck, a small room on either side of the smokestack, dubbed the "library" by passengers. The rooms are most often filled with commuters deeply engrossed in novels, crossword puzzles, or unfinished business from the office. (Courtesy of Khristopher La Plante.)

Bathed in chilly sunlight, the promenade deck of the *Wenatchee* still attracts commuters even in the depths of winter. Nowhere on the Sound will you find a better place to catch some welcome sun than on the deck of a WSF ferry. (Photograph by the author.)

Commuters and tourists alike appreciate the long bench seats next to the windows on the *Wenatchee*. Many of the seats have tables to either work, eat, or play a game of cards over while Mount Rainier and the scenery drift past outside. Few ferry commuters would ever trade their mode of transportation, happy to relax while others are stuck in traffic along I-5. (Photograph by the author.)

The third of the Mark II trio is the *Puyallup*. Perhaps the best of the three, the ferry has been a permanent resident of the Edmonds-Kingston run since joining the fleet in 1999. The ferry runs so smoothly, it is sometimes difficult to tell when the engines have engaged and the vessel is underway. (Photograph by the author.)

Some of the advantages the Mark II's have over other vessels in the fleet are the wider stairwells and passages. While not the same kind of "grand staircase" built into the *Kalakala*, the *Puyallup* and other Mark II's have simple but pleasing entryways nonetheless. (Photograph by the author.)

As it is being chased by seagulls, the mammoth *Puyallup* approaches the dock. (Courtesy of Khristopher LaPlante.)

The first of a new generation of fast passenger-only ferries, the *Chinook* went into service in 1998. An immediate hit with commuters, the fast, comfortable ferry cut commute time to Bremerton in half. (Photograph by the author.)

Shown here at full speed in Rich Passage at around 34 knots, the *Chinook* heads for Bremerton. Unfortunately, it wasn't to last. Lawsuits were filed and the fast ferries slowed before they could show their true potential. Wake has been an issue in Rich Passage since the appearance of the *Indianapolis* and *Chippewa* in 1910. The *Chinook* and the *Snohomish* are Chinook class vessels, built by Dakota Creek Industries of Anacortes, Washington, in 1998 and 1999. They measure 143 feet, 3 inches by 39 feet, 4 inches and are powered by diesel water jet propulsion. (Photograph by the author.)

It is launch day for the *Snohomish*, sister to the *Chinook*. At the time, an ambitious program to provide fast, passenger-only service from Kingston to Seattle and from Southworth and Vashon to Seattle, in addition to Bremerton, was underway. Unfortunately, the next election would cut funding for the program. (Courtesy of Jean P. Hudson.)

With champagne smashed across her bow, the *Snohomish* is christened. Even though the passenger-only boats are the smallest in the fleet, when shown to scale with the passengers they will carry the boats are still quite large. (Courtesy of Jean P. Hudson.)

Out of the barn, the *Snohomish* is moved closer to water for the first time. (Courtesy of Jean P. Hudson.)

The *Snohomish* is now officially a ferry, floating in salt water for the first time. The 350-passenger vessel was slightly larger than her sister, due to a bow modification that would allow her to dock at the auto ramps as well as the passenger-only slip. (Courtesy of Jean P. Hudson.)

The *Snohomish* is shown here tied up at Bremerton on one of her last runs to the city. Washington State Ferry passenger-only service to Bremerton was discontinued in 2003. Today, the *Chinook* and the *Snohomish* are moored in Eagle Harbor, facing an uncertain future. (Photograph by the author.)